Technology Enterprise Business Models: A Handbook For The Post Pandemic Era

Authored by

Joosung J. Lee

Enterprise School,
Soonchunhyang University, Asan,
South Korea

Technology Enterprise Business Models: A Handbook For The Post Pandemic Era

Author: Joosung J. Lee

ISBN (Online): 978-981-5179-48-4

ISBN (Print): 978-981-5179-49-1

ISBN (Paperback): 978-981-5179-50-7

First published in 2023.

need for a court order if at any point you breach any terms of this License Agreement. In no event will any delay or failure by Bentham Science Publishers in enforcing your compliance with this License Agreement constitute a waiver of any of its rights.

3. You acknowledge that you have read this License Agreement, and agree to be bound by its terms and conditions. To the extent that any other terms and conditions presented on any website of Bentham Science Publishers conflict with, or are inconsistent with, the terms and conditions set out in this License Agreement, you acknowledge that the terms and conditions set out in this License Agreement shall prevail.

Bentham Science Publishers Pte. Ltd.
80 Robinson Road #02-00
Singapore 068898
Singapore
Email: subscriptions@benthamscience.net

BENTHAM SCIENCE

CONTENTS

PREFACE

To offer a new service in business, technologies are often used to increase efficiency and service quality. Over the past few years, the service industry has transformed itself to adapt to the fast-changing business environment and consumer demand. Global industrial and educational activities are fast changing to adjust to the new paradigms caused by the COVID-19 pandemic. New business models that incorporate innovative technologies and deliver online-offline hybrid services are necessary to continue generating economic value. Technology servitization strategies are important in order to create valuable innovations for both conventional and new industries. This short book equips students and entrepreneurs with the following capabilities:

1. Value creation methods based on the holistic value chain of manufacturing and service convergence

2. Service management basics from new service design including customer journey map analysis to designing effective online-offline blended business models.

3. Insights into new business plan making along with a variety of latest innovative cases through the pandemic era.

Joosung J. Lee

Enterprise School,
Soonchunhyang University, Asan,
South Korea

ACKNOWLEDGEMENTS

This research was supported by Soonchunhyang University's research project #2021-0922.The author also acknowledges the students' assistance in preparing the manuscript.

CHAPTER 1

Introduction to Technology-Service Management: Servitization, Frameworks, and Servitization Trends

Abstract: How to turn a traditional product into a service? How to equip the existing physical medium with differentiating features? Why do we need complementary services to an already seemingly efficient product? These and many more are the questions that concern the area of Technology-Service Management - the field, that primarily deals with the idea of developing and implementing technology for the sake of creating a service-shaped value out of it.

In this chapter, we will become familiar with the ever-evolving definition of servitization and understand why innovative firms are interested in pursuing this strategy. Subsequently, the chapter will introduce two necessary frameworks for identifying the need for servitization - namely, the Gap Model of Service Quality and ServQual. Finally, we will explore three types of Product-Service Systems (PSS) through the case studies of the recent servitization trends.

Keywords: Gap model, Product-service systems, Product-as-a-service, Service quality, servitization.

INTRODUCTION: THE CONCEPT OF SERVITIZATION

In such a large field covering numerous aspects related to services, the concept of *servitization* stands especially strong, continuing to develop both in academic and industrial realms in the current highly digitised business landscape. As entrepreneurial organisations all over the world began releasing the value of intangible offerings, *servitization*, has established its roots in even the most traditional markets long before academic interest in it. One of the examples of the first industrial servitization initiative belongs to Rolls Royce and their "power-by-the-hour" trademark, which was developed in 1962 (Rolls-Royce, 2012). Then-radical approach to simply leasing out an aerospace engine on an hourly basis with complementary mechanic services instead of selling it to airlines became the new business-deal standard in the industry making it easier for airlines to sustain the existing and acquire the newest additions to their aeroparks. Servitization, then, in its purest form can be generally identified as *an innovative strategy of adding services to the already offered physical goods in order to gain market competitiveness and customer turnover.*

However, the notion of servitization has continued to evolve and has gained many shapes. Transforming from the simplest combined form of physical products and intangible services, servitization now represents *a complex strategy of highly customised solutions pursued in hopes of achieving higher customer satisfaction.* Still, the core of servitization, based on the pursuit of the combination of *goods, services and support*, remains the same. For instance, the solutions, which many of us cannot imagine modern life without, such as Netflix, Uber and Spotify all come together under the umbrella term of servitization initiatives. As such, the firms deploy personalised services and products, which ensure connected, long-term relationships with customers, hence, foster business profitability.

BENEFITS OF SERVITIZATION

Fig. (1). The Main Reasons for Companies to Implement Servitization.

As can be seen from the examples drawn before, servitization is first and foremost an essentially beneficial strategy for firms, who rely solely on supplying hardware products (Fig. **1**). Adapting the strategies of Product-Service System (PSS) or Product-as-a-Service (PaaS), manufacturers, such as Rolls Royce, are able to not simply differentiate their revenue streams and improve product innovation, but more importantly - suggest thoroughly customised approaches to the consumer (Emerald Publishing, 2022). In this sense, servitization covers every vital aspect of a customer's journey by prolonging trust-based interaction between the firm and the client from the stages of actual purchase up until even the disposal of the product. For example, one of the leading Korean car manufacturers, Hyundai

Motor Company, has undertaken an innovative solution in servitization by initiating proprietary remanufacturing and service stations for "recovering mechanical sub-assemblies". This way, Hyundai is now responsible for satisfying the customer along the whole journey, finishing up with the recycling and reusing run-down parts as new materials for further construction. This servitization ensures Hyundai is able to continue prospering within the new sustainable type of circular economy as the innovative player in the car market.

Servitization, then, enhances both business and social welfare by accentuating the consumption of a business outcome instead of the simple and rather ecologically daunting purchase and disposal of equipment. In this scenario, the new unconventional business models of online businesses that we mentioned earlier, based purely on sharing and consumption of outcomes, are some of the most radical forms of servitization, which ensure zero-waste production.

The gradual transition to a more outcome-based PSS mode has also proven to be an advantageous tactic during the COVID-19 pandemic in specific, when "intangible assets", *services*, maximised corporate resilience for innovative businesses. This and other Technology-Service Business Innovations through the Pandemic Era will be discussed in detail in Chapter 2.

IDENTIFYING THE NEED FOR SERVITIZATION: YANDEX'S PSS

Now that we have underlined the numerous advantages of pursuing servitization strategy, it is important to understand *how* a firm is able to identify the need for it - through what tools and frameworks a business can approach the question of whether to implement it or not.

Although servitization is often highlighted as a desirable and often essential plan of action, this is not to say that it is always the final right answer for all businesses. For example, an innovative company Xerox, although having started pursuing servitization strategy, eventually had to separate its service and product businesses. Such a process is referred to as *deservitization*, when firms step away from service-oriented initiatives due to either failure in handling PSS models or the decision to further broaden and diversify their services, which are no longer as tightly related to their physical goods.

The Gap Model of Service Quality

Then, the question that arises is: how can entrepreneurs recognize the need for better servitization in their specific case? To do this, in 1985 Parasuraman, Zeithaml and Berry developed a framework called the *Gap Model of Service Quality*.

However, before diving deeper into the framework of the Gap Model, it is essential to understand the notions of service and quality separately. *Service* is usually perceived as something attributed as intangible, inseparable, heterogeneous, and perishable (Table 1).

Table 1. The Four Characteristics of Service.

	Concept	Example: Taxi Service
Intangibility	Unlike a product, a service does not have a physical presence. Service consists of processes and results of actions.	The process of driving does not have a physical presence.
Inseparability	The production of a service cannot be separated from the consumption of a service because the service is consumed as it is delivered.	The production of a taxi service (=driving) cannot be separated from its consumption (=riding).
Heterogeneity	All services are unique. The same service may contain a different value depending on who provides a service when, where, and how.	Customers receive different values from a taxi service. A taxi driver can be either kind or rude. Traffic jams can also decrease the value of a taxi service.
Perishability	Unlike a product, a service quickly diminishes and it cannot be stored for later use.	The taxi service exists only when a customer is in need of a ride - once the need is gone, there is no longer any value of a taxi service for this specific customer.

Based on this understanding of service, it is easy to recognize the value of quality associated with a service as quality largely reflects the gap between the intended idea of service and the actual outcome offered. In this sense, the Service Gaps Model can help the business understand what kind of challenges may taint their customers' satisfaction and how these issues namely arise. The Service Gaps Model proposes that the more efficiently the expectations of the customer are met, the more satisfied with the service the customer will eventually be. This is a useful tool for recognizing the need for pursuing servitization strategy or changing its direction.

The five gaps in the service quality are created with five elements in the process of providing the service to customers. The expected service that the customer possesses is basically made from the verbal communication among them, the pain points, or the related-past experience of a similar service. Before approaching the final communication between the service provider and the consumer, the business goes through the process of market research, while designing the service and dealing with the standard of service quality. Passing through all the elements, finally, the service could be reached by the customers, who form their own perception of the outcome consumed, which may either differ or coincide with the firm's own intentions.

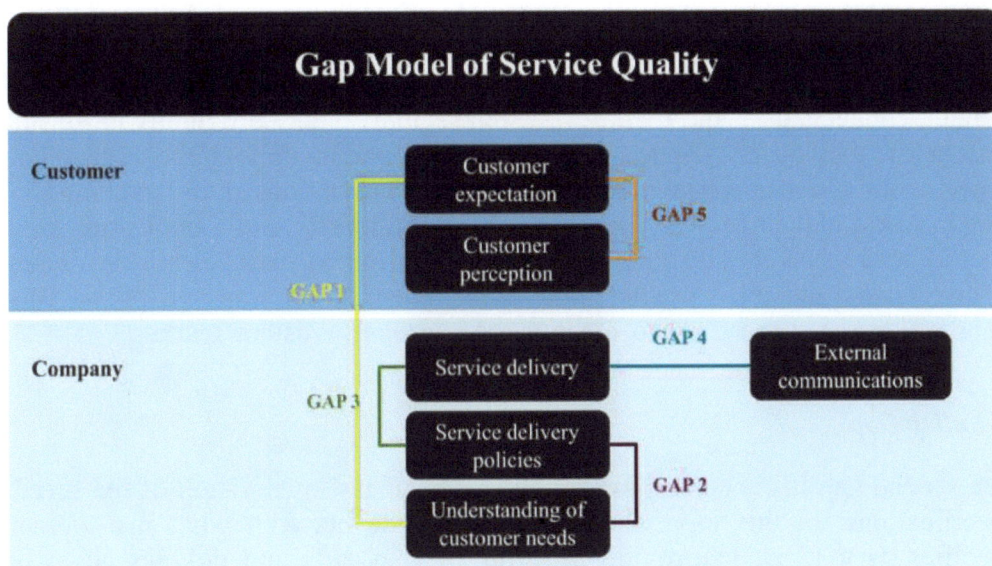

Fig. (2). Areas Where Service Gaps Occur.

In this Chapter, the Service Quality Gap Model in Fig. (**2**) will be represented and analysed based on the case study of the Russian internet company, Yandex, and their implementation of the Product-Service system in pursuit of closing the 5 service quality gaps. It is especially helpful to overview the given framework through the PSS initiative of Yandex to understand how efficient closure of the Gaps can lead to a successful servitization initiative, which results in higher customer satisfaction and differentiation of a firm's core businesses.

1. Knowledge Gap

This type of gap usually results from the difference between what customers expect to receive as a service and what business sees as customers' expectations. The main problem, in this case, stands in the managerial unawareness of customers' needs. Some of the major potential causes of such incompetence can be the lack of interaction between the company and the client and, most importantly, insufficient market research. Overall, it signifies the inability of the company to acknowledge the existing and arising demands of the market and their customer's pain points. In order to close this first gap, it is essential to conduct market research in a meticulous manner and get customers' feedback to analyse it and add demanded aspects, while getting rid of the unnecessary or potentially harmful ones.

In the case of Yandex (2022), the *Knowledge Gap* could open if the users were expecting the company to come up with an AI speaker and assistant, but Yandex's management would have been unaware of such need in the market. However, as Yandex conducts user and market research regularly, they efficiently close such gaps before they occur. Yandex is exceptionally good in aligning their customers' expectations and managerial perception of those expectations since the company's core business is their search engine - the in-state alternative of Google, much like South Korea's Naver. The data received from unlimited searches allows Yandex to understand and even predict their users' needs. This was one of the ways Yandex identified the need to enter the AI speaker-assistant market.

2. Policy Gap

The second gap is concerned more with the business' own vision of the service specifications. In this case, there is a difference between what management specifies as to what to provide in terms of standards and policies and what management thinks the customers' expectations are. The reasons for such a gap can be the insufficient communication between different service levels, as well as the inability to regularly update service level standards. To assure the closure of this gap, the business has to specify clearly what kind of service the customers will receive, as well as make sure that the specifications are transferred to clients in a clear manner.

For Yandex, it was especially crucial to ensure that the quality of their innovative product and service of the AI assistant were up to managerial perceptions of customers' expectations. In the worst case scenario of the *Policy Gap* occurrence, it would have been the events of when Yandex offered both the AI speaker and assistant, but the quality of the sound speaker would have been too unsatisfactory.

3. Delivery Gap

The delivery gap is also often related to miscommunication between different levels of management when the service specifications are not clearly expressed and delivered and the actual outcome of the service does not reflect the policies and standards put in it. It is usually caused by the failure of matching supply and demand, unsolved major problems in HR and disturbed teamwork among separate management and development levels. To avoid the emergence of this gap, a firm can implement mixed workshops to ensure stable communication between different layers of the company, provide training for its employees and conduct regular team meetings.

The *Delivery Gap* should be checked for internal processes within the organisation as there should be smooth connection between different managerial and engineering layers of the company. In this event, there would be a difference between Yandex's specification of what the AI assistant should be able to do and what Alice can actually do - meaning that some of the unrealistic standards for the AI assistant should be checked for future implementation equal to the scope of resources available. Yandex efficiently closed this gap by postponing the availability of such a feature as personal identification. This is to say that the AI assistant is yet to be able to recognize its user by voice only and the assistant cannot save up all the information received to make a whole portrait of the user to predict their future needs.

4. Communication Gap

The *Communication Gap* is one of the common ones as every company strives to market itself as being the most innovative. In this case, the gap signifies the difference between what is promised in the promotion and what actually gets delivered as an outcome. Businesses that are inclined towards falling into this gap are usually the overachieving firms, which rely on unrealistic directions of the management team and cannot establish direct communication channels between the PR team and the operations team. Some of the possible solutions for filling this gap could be improving internal communication between technical, marketing and operation teams. This gap is one of the most crucial ones to close as it directly leads to the dissatisfaction of the customers with the service they receive.

As such, it was also in the best interests of Yandex not to over-promote both Yandex Station and the assistant as highly futuristic developments in order to avoid promises overtaking the image of the actual product and service. In this sense, Yandex's PR team was taking highly calculated steps when describing the abilities of their new products and the communication team was referring to Yandex.Station as "a work in progress". It was crucial to not let impossible expectations spread among the users as Yandex still had powerful and arguably more innovative rivals, such as Amazon's Alexa and Google's Assistant.

5. Customer Gap

The final *Customer Gap* is the one solely depending on the customers' side. It has to deal with the high distinction between the expected service and the received service. Arguably, it is the most crucial gap as some of the businesses are unaware of this gap occurring in regard to their offerings as it mainly occurs externally to the firm. It is valuable to get informed of this gap through direct communication channels: forums, feedback sections or the book of complaints and suggestions. The importance of this gap also stands in the fact that the only way to actually close it is to fulfill all the previous four gaps.

In the case of Yandex, eventually, by taking care of all the previous gaps, the *Customer Gap* has been ultimately closed down. As this gap mainly occurs if the customers are unaware of what exactly the service should be and often misunderstand the quality, it has been essential for Yandex to manage this gap efficiently by aligning customers' expectations and customers' perceptions. Both Yandex.Station and Alice became one of the most successful PSS implemented in the industry. By closing down all the potential gaps in service quality, Yandex ensured its high position in the market having a rating of 91% of satisfied reviews at Yandex's original marketplace.

THE SERVQUAL MODEL

There are five dimensions, which are used to evaluate the quality of the service offered to customers and are referred to as the SERVQUAL model. If those dimensions are all satisfied, it could be suggested that the consumer receives a high-quality service, which perfectly addresses all his needs and pain points. The five dimensions are as follows: Tangibles, Reliability, Responsiveness, Assurance, and Empathy. The below chart includes the explanation and examples of each dimension of the SERVQUAL framework (Table **2**).

Table 2. The Five Areas of Service Quality Assessment.

	Concept	Example
Tangibles	The physical objects included in the service.	• Whether the materials all have their own purpose, excluding useless components. • Whether the physical facilities, equipment, personnel, and any materials used for the service are visually well-organised.
Reliability	How many promises between service providers and receivers are kept.	• Whether the services are provided on time with the accurate supplies. • Whether the services are based on the promised compositions targeting the customer. • Whether the provider is dependable enough to properly respond toward unexpected problems.

(Table 2) cont.....

	Concept	Example
Responsiveness	The willingness of responding to customers' signs.	• Whether the provider is interested in the customers' request to promptly respond • Whether the service is flexible enough to inform and change its response based on the customers' demand.
Assurance	The trust based on the desirable attitudes customers could feel from the providers and service.	• Whether the service provider cares customers' feeling of safety and trust to keep using the service. • Whether the providers' attitude is in polite manners to encourage customers' action. • Whether the service itself is away from the potential or disclosed threats.
Empathy	Attention toward individual customers to understand better for more convenience.	• Whether the service providers could create personalised relationship with the customers based on the individuals' needs. • Whether the service providers care and do listen to the customers' situation such as setting convenient time schedules for customers. • Whether the service is based on the understanding of the customers.

Overall, it can be concluded that in order to stay afloat in the competitive business environment, an innovative organisation ought to close the service-quality gaps or at least minimise them, as well as satisfy all five dimensions of the SERVQUAL model. The Gap and SERVQUAL models are both useful tools for recognizing the "missing part" of the customer journey, which can attribute the decision of pursuing the servitization strategy.

TYPES OF SERVITIZATION

As we have learned to recognize the need for servitization, it is important to understand exactly which type of PSS system a firm not simply can, but should pursue in their specific case.

We have previously learned that a Product-Service System (PSS) is a marketable set of products and services that combines them in a modular and coherent manner to yield a greater overall value than a single product or service system. It was originally developed for conventional manufacturing companies to overcome the limit of product-only revenue models as it allows them to differentiate their offerings and also earn a continuous stream of revenue. This is called a Product-Oriented PSS. The core characteristic is that it is an augmentation of existing product-only systems with additional related services.

However, as PSS evolved, companies were founded entirely on the concept of a harmonious mix of products and services to focus on usage and the result rather than the product. In other words, PSS started from the far left on the PS scale represented above and began to move to the right, increasingly towards complete service-oriented models. Such Use-Oriented and Result-Oriented PSS' are more generally recognised as an innovation strategy for any firm across any industry. By only making use of the core values of a physical product and an intangible service, they offer innovative new business models and sources of revenue for the businesses, more efficient and hassle-free ways to complete a task for consumers, and even yield better outcomes for the society and the environment as was discussed earlier.

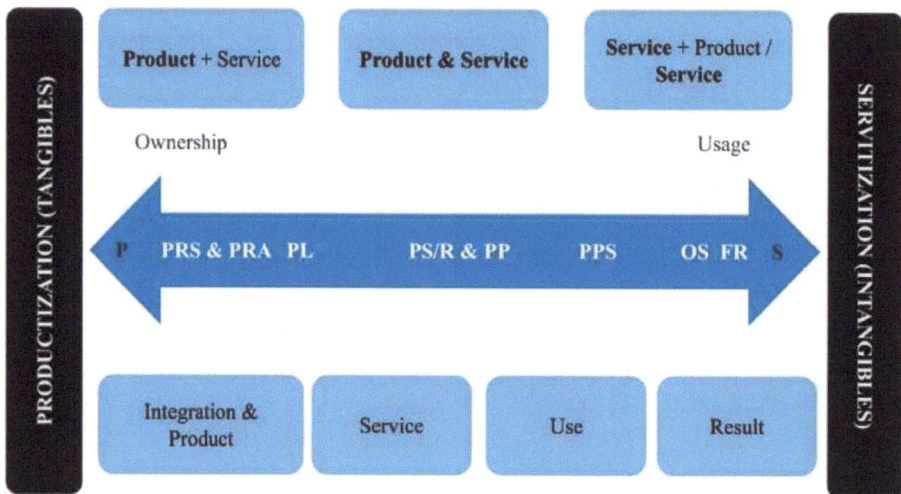

Fig. (3). Product-Service System (PSS) Combinations.

As such, there are three main categories of Product-Service Systems: *Product-Oriented*, *Use-Oriented* and *Result-Oriented*. Each category can be further divided into subcategories of PSS (Fig. **3**).

Product Oriented PSS: Product-Related Service (PRS) and Product-Related Advice (PRA)

On the far left of the PS scale are Product-Oriented services - the most traditional modes of selling the ownership of physical goods, but with a hint of innovative additional services. Product-Oriented services typically include recurring maintenance services and contracts, financing schemes, and supply of consumable complementary products, which provide continuous streams of revenue for the companies. One example of such a Product-Oriented model is Hyundai Motor Company's remanufacturing and service stations for "recovering mechanical sub-assemblies" that we covered at the beginning of the chapter.

Product-Related Services (PRS) can also include a contract-based ownership of a product, where the product is taken back to the provider after the contract expires. For instance, water dispenser services in South Korea provide regular maintenance and ownership of the product for a monthly fee. Such contract-based ownership is especially applicable for physical products, which are used for a long period of time, need regular care and replacement of consumables or consumable parts (*e.g.*, filters in water dispensers), or are mission-critical to daily business operations. Yandex's AI assistant can be also viewed through the lens of a PRS PSS, where the assistant is a complementary service to Yandex's hardware speaker.

In addition, a Product-Oriented PSS can focus on helping the customer get the most out of a physical product. In this case, it can be considered a Product-Related Advice service (PRA). A consumer electronics manufacturer, in addition to merely selling the physical product, can sell a set of courses that teach the customer how to make smart use of all the features of the product.

Use Oriented PSS: Product Lease, Product Sharing / Renting, Product Pooling and Pay-Per-Service

On the right of the Product-Oriented PSS is the Use-Oriented strategy. Here, the traditional physical product is still involved, but the revenue does not come simply from selling its ownership. The ownership remains in the hands of the service provider, and the product is used by consumers in various ways or even shared by multiple users.

Product Lease (PL) is the most traditional model of Use-Oriented service. One of the common examples of a PL PSS is a car market, where leasing vehicles is a common occurrence. Take the well-known Rolls Royce's "power-by-the-hour" strategy, for instance: while an airline does not technically own the product, it is very close to ownership as it utilises the airbuses regularly. An airline, in this case, has unlimited and exclusive access to the entire aircraft, and is also responsible for the maintenance, repair, and control just like an owner would be. The only difference is a lessee gives up a regular fee to the renter for the full use of the product instead of paying the full market price for owning it.

Product Renting or Sharing (PR/S) gears more toward usage than ownership. The user only pays for a short-lived usage of a product. It is the service provider that oversees maintenance, repair, and control of the product unlike in the PL model. Moreover, the product is often shared by multiple users. The most prominent example of a PR/S PSS is Uber, where customers only pay for a driving service for a short-lived period of time.

Product Pooling (PP) is largely similar to the PR/S PSS. To be more precise, Product Pooling is a subset of product renting and sharing. While the PR/S model includes services that are used one at a time by multiple users, PP services are used by multiple users at the same time. In South Korea, a prominent example of Product Pooling is the business model of Half and Half Taxi, where multiple customers are able to share a taxi ride simultaneously to divide the fee.

Pay-Per-Service (PPS) PSS model defines the value provided to the customer precisely in terms of a unit output of the product according to the user level. For instance, for lighting charge - it would be pay-per-lux, while for tires - pay-per-kilometre. This is especially useful for products, which have an irregular pattern of use or require a large initial investment for ownership. For businesses, it lowers the barriers to entry for potential customers, who do not have a sufficient use case for a product to acquire absolute ownership over it. The PPS PSS also often involves the complementary service of maintenance and care, transferring the burden that is associated with ownership to the service provider.

Result Oriented: Outsourcing and Functional Result

On the far right of the PS scale is the Result-Oriented services. The customer and the provider define the value purely based on the outcome. The business is free to use multiple products to deliver the outcome based on the context, and the customer does not get to choose the mechanism and the type of products that the provider decides to use, only caring about the final result.

The traditional mode of the Result-Oriented PSS is Outsourcing (OS), where a firm uses another firm's ability to deliver a result, which is necessary for their own business. The client firm at most provides performance indicators to control the quality of the outsourced service. The most general examples of an OS model include services such as manufacturing, food catering, and office cleaning.

The Functional Result (FR) PSS model is a more innovative type of servitization. The result can be achieved in a variety of ways through the usage of a variety of technologies and mechanisms. In this case, the customer is essentially only interacting with the outcome – the final result of all the mechanisms' work. To draw the distinctive difference between the FR and the Pay-Per-Service Use-

Oriented explained before, the user in the PPS environment already has control over which mechanism to use to obtain the said result. For example, the customer can choose to use a photocopier to get a physical copy of a file or a solar panel to generate renewable energy. In the Functional Result PSS, the user only receives the final outcome, but presumably does not care about the ways it was achieved. The most well-known example of such a Functional Result model can be Netflix and Spotify, where the user simply interacts with the result of the service - media in the form of either movies, TV shows or music, while the service provider is responsible for acquiring the products and delivering them.

CONCLUSION

In chapter 1, we have become familiar with the concept of servitization, its benefits, and the many faces of Product-Service Systems, which surround us in the most conventional and innovative markets. Through the cases of leading companies, such as Yandex, Hyundai Motor Company and Uber we were able to detect and understand in detail how, nowadays, the concept of servitization prevails to be an essential integrated part of even the most product-focused firms. Finally, we have identified two useful frameworks for recognizing the need for pursuing PSS systems and discussed the variety of types of Product-Service systems.

REFERENCES

Emerald Publishing. (2022). What is servitization of manufacturing? A quick introduction. *Emerald Publishing*. Available From: https://www.emeraldgrouppublishing.com/opinion-and-blog/what-servitizat-on-manufacturing-a-quick-introductionAccessed on February 14

Royce, R. Rolls-Royce celebrates 50th anniversary of Power-by-the-Hour. Available From: https://www.rolls-royce.com/media/press-releases-archive/yr-2012/121030-the-hour.aspxAccessed on February 23

Yandex.Market Reviews. Should I buy Yandex.Station? Available From: https://market.yandex.ru/product--umnaia-kolonka-yandex-stantsiia/1971204201/reviewsAccessed on March 10

CHAPTER 2

Technology-Service Business Innovations through the Pandemic Era

Abstract: In this Chapter, we will overview the cases of business innovation with a focus on servitization and digitization. The Chapter will introduce innovative initiatives in traditional markets, such as health and medicine-related, as well as manufacturing spheres. Lastly, we will become familiar with more unconventional pandemic-induced innovations within the clothing retail and fitness industries.

Keywords: Digitalization, Remote service, Sustainable servitization, Telemedicine, Virtual health.

INTRODUCTION

As has been largely implied throughout Chapter I, the gradual transition to a more outcome-based PSS mode has also proven to be an advantageous tactic during the COVID-19 pandemic in specific, when "intangible assets", and *services*, maximised corporate resilience for innovative businesses. Not only business initiatives in the healthcare sector, primarily focused on delivering essential for survival non-face-to-face medicine practices, but, in fact, every single non-physical intangible solution, which could be easily distributed in a suddenly dispersed and distanced world, has gained, as what industries believe, "overnight success".

The pandemic has become the break-open door for new market entry and, in many ways, its disruption by previously considered unconventional and risky players, who had struggled with staying afloat against the existing "traditional" corporations or setting up a legit foundation for the new market offer. While some of the traditional business giants have shown struggles adapting to the new reality of the closed-off world and the "new normal" of creating an online presence, easily accessible even through the harsh limitations, a number of innovative new firms have actively started taking over the decades-long set positions of industry standards.

Such a window of opportunities was majorly contributed to by the pandemic rules, dictating humanity to adopt solutions to retain their old familiar lifestyle, while existing in the brand new unexpected reality. Besides the apparent COVID-19-related health struggles, the pandemic has been proven to be especially harsh on the disabled community and other people with already pre-existing health conditions, such as diabetes. Patients, who had previously been under constant control, management, and physical care of health facilities and caretakers, were suddenly urged to attend to their own needs and learn to self-manage their conditions.

In addition to special struggles, such ordinary activities as meeting other people, having work meetings, attending school, stocking up on groceries and even doing a regular workout became a challenge in the new normal of self-isolation, causing the growth of mental health issues and further complication of already existing physical barriers. As such, not simply each industry, but the whole world was in urgent need of everyday solutions for a previously *normal undisturbed* lifestyle. Servitization trend with a core focus on digitalization and sustainability, then, became the *new standard for the new normal*.

In this Chapter, we will overview the cases of business innovation with the focus on servitization and digitization. The chapter will introduce innovative initiatives in traditional markets, such as health and medicine-related, as well as manufacturing spheres. Lastly, we will become familiar with more unconventional pandemic-induced innovations within the clothing retail and fitness industries.

SERVITIZATION: DIGITALIZATION AND SUSTAINABILITY TAKING OVER THE PANDEMIC

The pandemic has made the question of pursuing integrated digital-based solutions, consisting of not simply a physical offer but also an intangible online-transmitted part of service, more crucial than ever (Fig. **4**). As many firms have already been engaging in distancing themselves from strict productization and approaching the right side of the PSS spectrum, some were still reluctant to pursue even a partial transition to digital online platforms to provide and advertise their services. The pandemic, however, completely ruled out such hesitation and debunked the myth of the online bubble.

74% of firms have engaged in creation of digital operating models

70% of firms have initiated creation of new digital business models and revenue streams

74% of firms have engaged in creation of digital operating models

75% of firms started the transition to digital seamless customer experience

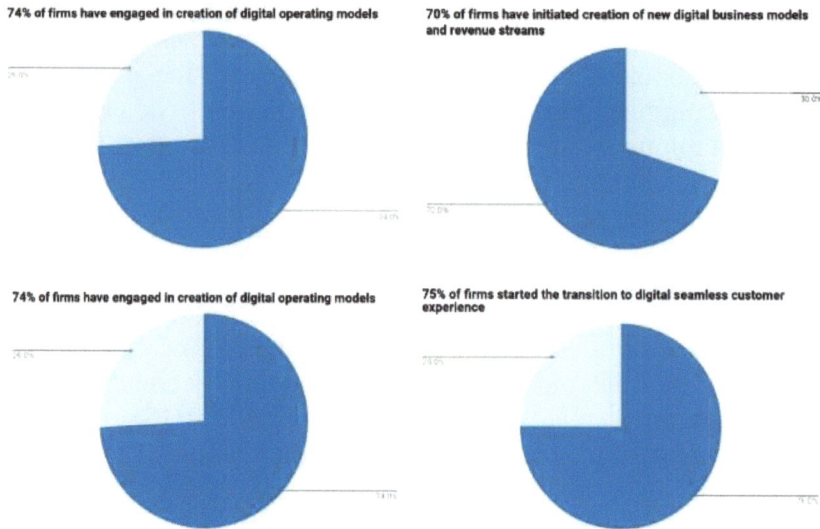

Fig. (4). Digital Transformation Accelerated by the Pandemic.

Servitization of the existing business models, in this sense, became the right step towards a more digitalized and sustainable operation. Digitalization has started accelerating "by months or even years" at its normal speed due to the COVID-19 pandemic and is here to stay even after the pandemic is over. This includes not only the digital transformation of operating models but also providing seamless digital customer experience and increasing the workforce through new ways of remote, AI-driven and automation opportunities. Although there are certain challenges to the complete transition to the digital realm of providing products and services, such as lack of knowledge and resources capacity, the majority of the innovative firms are continuing to diligently invest in the development and acquisition of tools, which can help them to "help both customers and workers".

Similarly, self-isolation has highlighted on the sustainability trend or more so the radical need for it in primarily physically present industries. The pandemic not only brought to light the essential front-line position of the lower-class workers, such as waste collectors and cleaners, but also taught all the sectors the harsh lesson of planning, preparing, and mobilising resources in advance. The listed initiatives and key messages are perfectly aligned with the ideas of integrated PSS solutions targeted at reducing the continuous production of new goods and increasing the sharing of the philosophy of already existing products. Moreover, as will be discussed later in detail in the section of the chapter on manufacturing servitization, digital-oriented servitization provides crucial insights into the ways the currently existing products and services are organised and consumed by the users through the automation processes and data-driven operating models. This perfectly synchronyzed way of managing operations is what allows product-oriented firms to ensure the necessary planning and mobilisation of the resources, which is crucial for sustaining the *green* initiatives of such firms.

HEALTH- AND MEDICINE-RELATED INNOVATIONS

Evidently, however, the first industry, which was urged to engage in speedy yet necessary transition to digital servitization was the health and medicine sector. The demand for non-face-to-face treatment and medical consultations reached their peak during the pandemic as people were seeking ways to ensure the stability of both their mental and physical conditions in a restricted out-of-reach world. As mentioned in the opening remarks of the chapter, the interest in virtual sessions with specialists has skyrocketed not only among patients with already pre-existing medical conditions but within the whole society as the COVID anxiety surged. To be more specific, the demand for virtual medical sessions became more than double by 2021 in comparison to its 2015 rate, clearly indicating the abrupt leap in the demand for remote online-based doctor appointments. For example, the dramatic growth of online medical sessions, conducted through video conferencing tools, was especially noticeable in the sector of psychotherapy as non-face-to-face appointments became more common and "are here to stay" with almost 60% of the US residents switching to online sessions during the pandemic without a substantial negative effect on the effectiveness or quality of the medical consultations (Pancani, 2021).

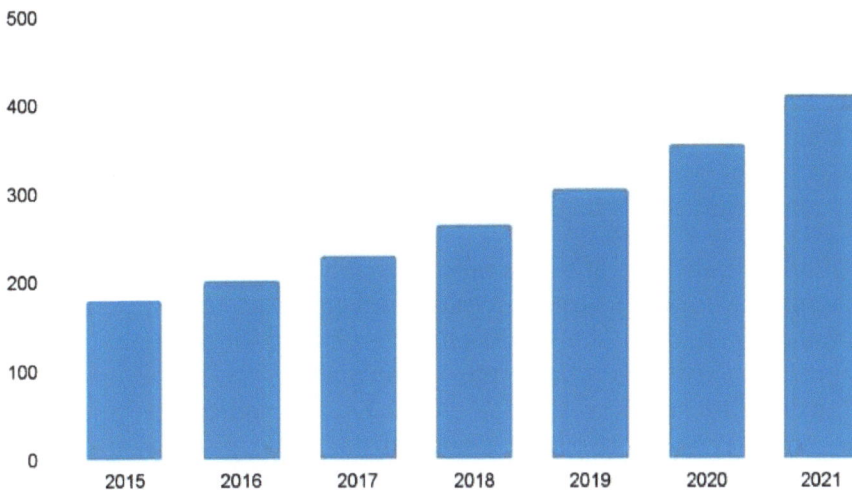

Fig. (5). Fast Growing Global Telemedicine Market (in billion dollars).

However, such unnoticeable interest spiked not only the transition of individual doctor appointments to video-conferencing tools, such as Zoom but also greatly affected other more unconventional digital health sectors, such as telemedicine or telehealth, medical control and management applications, platforms and physical wearables for tracking health conditions and diseases (Fig. **5**).

Telehealth: Virtual Platforms for Medical Consultations

Among the innovative digital servitization initiatives, telehealth, a more convenient way for consumers to access and increase self-care, has become one of the standards. In the first four months of 2020 only, the number of online medical appointments has increased by more than 50%. As such, the market of telehealth or telemedicine, despite its numerous challenges and limitations, is expected to reach over $180 billion by the year of 2026 due to its numerous benefits. The most advantageous of them are listed as significantly reducing the number of office visits by around 15% and travel time for a patient by over 100 minutes, while maximising the chance of providing timely medical assistance (Koonin *et al.*, 2020).

While the more traditional approach to providing healthcare remained within the frames of the video conferencing softwares, one of the leading professional therapy providers TalkSpace supplied mental help via a proprietary platform, which was "built for a moment like this pandemic". Based on the recent findings that patients can still form tight bonds with therapists without ever hearing or seeing them personally, TalkSpace offers video, sound and even text services for patients and therapists to choose an individually suitable format of sessions from. Such a connector platform has become a beneficial digital initiative to promote the labour standards of therapists, who are often underpaid and overworked by offline workplaces, as well as an advantageous deal for patients, who are able to receive essential mental help remotely. TalkSpace has become the largest player in the virtual therapy industry, raising over $100 million of funding and helping therapists and patients find each other in the unprecedented times of the non-face-to-face mental healthcare industry shift (Pierce, 2020).

Among similar innovative business models that have gained significant customer flow is Apollo 247, India's largest digital healthcare platform, which was founded by Dr. Prathap C. Reddy. The online clinic has been pioneering the telemedicine industry in India by providing "easily accessible" and "removing mobility barriers" healthcare services, such as online 1-on-1 medical consultation, online pharmacy and diagnosis accessible straight from home. By providing services in the digital format since 2021, Apollo 247 believes it significantly reduces the cost of a doctor visit for an average Indian, making medicine not only remotely accessible, but largely more affordable than standard medical appointments. To ensure their servitization catering not only to one-time customers, but also to patients in need of constant medical control and management, Apollo 247 launched a premium healthcare program under the name of CIRCLE. The premium membership offers patients with chronic conditions a chance to receive exclusive deals and constant control of their health status, making their conditions less burdensome management-wise.

In a similar manner, a Chinese smartphone app called Ping An Good Doctor has surpassed over 100 million users during the pandemic as the solution allowed customers to book and attend non-face-to-face medical consultations alongside receiving digital prescriptions. The innovative solution was especially helpful during the pandemic crisis in China as there was a dramatic shortage of medical human resources, which was burdened even more by harsh self-isolation restrictions. Following in the footsteps of its predecessor mobile platform Chun-Yi-Sheng, Ping An Good Doctor not only offers a range of already existing medical digital services, but is also hoping to build further capabilities with the usage of big data to enforce automated AI-powered healthcare consultations.

Automated Diagnosis Platforms and Applications

As can be seen from the example of Ping An Good Doctor, innovative technologies are continuing to be developed through the presence of machine learning and big data capabilities. Helping to increase the efficiency and accuracy of diagnosis and dealing with the issue of human resources shortage, automated diagnostics solutions have started growing alongside telemedicine.

One such data-driven initiative is Lunit INSIGHT CXR, a lung disease detection AI software developed in South Korea. It is a testing solution that analyzes a patient's chest X-ray image within a few seconds and automatically marks each suspected disease area, providing additional essential insights, such as the specific area, abnormality score and detailed report, for more correct diagnosis. The biggest advantage of Lunit INSIGHT CXR is its ability to detect major abnormalities, including lung nodules, hardening of the lungs and pneumothorax, with 97-99% accuracy in just a few seconds to ensure early and less expensive detection of more serious diseases, such as lung cancer, and giving a higher chance of survival to the patient.

Another diagnostic pandemic-related initiative undertaken by a large corporation was Apple's Siri assistance with aiding in pre-diagnosing COVID-19 symptoms. Through the additional voice command of "Siri, do I have the coronavirus?", Apple's Siri has been able to check whether the user is infected with the virus based on the questionnaire and data provided by the US Public Health Service and

CDC. In case the user is suspected to be positive by Siri, the voice assistant directs them to the approved telehealth services for more specific and accurate remote diagnosis and consultations without the additional risks of attending the offline clinic. This way, Apple is able to contribute directly to the timeliness and efficiency of the COVID-19 symptoms detection of their users by empowering their voice assistant's capability to access the necessary healthcare information and compare it to the user's symptoms in the shortest period of time.

Health Condition Tracking Software and Wearables

However, although a timely single diagnosis can prevent the negative development of a sudden illness, integrated health tracking solutions are considered to be more effective in the cases of chronic or long-term conditions, such as diabetes or ulcer, where constant control and management of vital body signals are essential. Previously, it has been a medical standard to attend regular check-up sessions with prescribed long-term doctors to ensure the satisfactory state of a patient's chronic condition with only a number of digital solutions for health tracking. However, the pandemic has become an unexpected but harsh push towards quick adaptation of such wearable or online solutions as face-to-face appointments became primarily unavailable.

One of such pandemic-driven business models has become Binah.ai, a B2B health data-driven AI-powered solution. Binah is able to track a wide range of wellness measurements, which are essential for health tracking, through a video-based machine and deep learning algorithms, which extract vital signs from the video picture and analyse them. The software is able to measure various vital rates and signals, such as heart rate variability, oxygen saturation, respiration rate, pulse and others in under one minute time. Based on this premise, Binah proposes a highly customised and cost-saving approach to health-tracking wearable companies, which can use Binah's proprietary technology through licensing.

Working alongside the mission of Binah, the Biofourmis platform offers a complete integrated solution accessible to healthcare providers, individual patients, and companies. The digitally powered wearable device utilises machine and deep learning techniques and FDA analytics to ensure the stable and continuous flow of patients' signals and their deterioration directly to care teams through smart notifications, giving both the patient and the medical staff a sense of health security even with the limited number of face-to-face check-ups. Such continuous control and delivery of real-time data also allow the company to use the stored data to foster the customised approach undertaken by pharmaceutical companies in providing complementary to their drug digital therapy.

SERVITIZING MANUFACTURING INDUSTRY

The disruption in the manufacturing sector has been seen as an inevitable consequence of the transition to less physically present industries during the pandemic. In the manufacturing sector, as the most traditional productization-oriented business model, in specific, servitization could be described as the "process of building revenue streams from services", where digital technologies and services have become the core of the mechanism's smooth work during the socially distanced period. As a result, manufacturing organisations with essential elements of servitization, including IoT, big data, cloud computing and predictive analytics have been able to rule out the possibility of failure during the pandemic and improve their resilience.

Essentially reliant on the continuous supply of globally scattered raw materials, the manufacturing industry has suffered significantly from the international logistics restrictions and subsequent shortage of resources in the first period of the pandemic. As such, it has become an essential question for firms that rely on the foreign supply of raw materials, to ensure uninterrupted manufacturing processes with limited resources and capabilities. Accordingly, those manufacturing organisations, who have begun investing in servitization and digitization initiatives before the pandemic hit, were able to rearrange their business and manufacturing operations according to the given limitations with the usage of data-driven predictive analytics and IoT embedded in their manufacturing standards.

Moreover, with the pandemic putting remote work into the spotlight, people became more reluctant to buy and actually own a car due to the lack of previously common long commuting problems. As such, a new flexible business model of car-as-a-service has been brought up with forecasts claiming that by 2025, 1 in 5 new cars will be offered *via* a subscription rather than ownership. For instance, such automobile manufacturing brands as Tesla, BMW, Porsche, Mercedes, and Volvo have started offering their products under a monthly subscription, maximising the usage of each consumable, the company's profit and reducing the manufacturing burden on the firm, while still satisfying the needs of the consumers to the best of their needs with the usage of complementary digital services empowered by big data and IoT.

SERVITIZATION TAKING THE NEXT STEP: CASES OF FITNESS, AND CLOTHING RETAIL INNOVATIONS

The self-isolation regulations and the new normal also brought massive reconstructive changes into the arguably daily necessities industries, such as clothing and fitness sectors. Although the undeniable digitalization of these industries has been present since the early 2010s with the growth of online marketplaces and proprietary stores, the pandemic has pushed the consumerism culture to yet another extreme, giving birth to the new level of the material world. Virtual consumerism of now almost unreachable goods and services has become a new method of self-therapy in unprecedented anxious times, where a contactless delivery made by a frontline worker was, perhaps, the only social interaction one could hope for in weeks. As such, a growing number of firms were in a hurry to engage in digital servitization to grab the benefits while they last.

Clothing Virtual Transformation Boom

The clothing retail industry has been identified as one of the most innovative players during the pandemic, which has been long prepared to transition to a majorly digitalized servitization model. Although fashion retailers were forced to temporarily discontinue their physical offline stores, causing abrupt massive financial losses, the apparel, fashion, and luxury industry has moved quickly towards digital transformation. Online servitization was necessary for not simply more efficient pandemic-struck operation management, but also to regenerate the dying demand for clothing as the period for setting up an online e-commerce platform shortened to as quickly as 13 weeks only.

Such fashion giants such as Dior, Tommy Hilfiger, Ralph Lauren, Balenciaga and Burberry, have opted for opening virtual stores amid the pandemic, utilising the technology of a leading software provider called Obsess. The platform allows retailers to generate 3D models of their physical stores to recreate the real-life shopping experience, claiming that over 70% of online visitors end up with a purchase. As such, on the wave of the distanced world and harsh restrictions, Obsesses has acquired funding of over $10 million in 2021 due to their innovative timely solution, which helped global leaders of the clothing and fashion industry overcome the offline crisis.

Similarly, one of the leading tech smartphone giants, Snapchat, has decided to launch a proprietary AR solution in partnership with such fashion brands as Farfetch and Prada Now, customers are able to try before they buy even without being physically present in a fitting room, almost perfectly imitating the real-life creases of fabric and movement *via* the usage of machine learning algorithms. Moreover, going hand in hand with size personalisation solutions, such as mybraFit, Snapchat is continuing to further improve their online automated virtual in-store consultancy regarding the right sizing of clothes. This way clothing brands are able to harvest the benefits of online try-ons without the additional expenses of sustaining a physical offline store, yet offer more customised and automated and still real-life-like service experience to their customers, which has become an essential driver in helping the clothing retail industry to avoid massive pandemic-inflicted fall.

Virtual Workouts as the New Go-To Standard

With the pandemic literally paralysing the active lifestyle of society, home workouts have become the only method of keeping oneself in shape. Although online workouts conducted through video-conferencing tools have reserved a high position among the solutions for the distancing rules, more innovative approaches, such as VR games for workouts have also paved the way into the everyday life of a person living through the pandemic.

One such solution was launched in April 2020 by the VR gaming industry leader, Oculus VR. Introducing "a new fun way to stay fit" right in the middle of worldwide self-isolation, the firm offered a full fitness package Supernatural that has become a massive success, getting thousands of positive reviews from people in need of activity stuck at home. With a simple headset, now, the user was able to not simply get their activity rate up and bring benefits to their health and body, but also find a way to entertain themselves as VR workouts consisted of unconventional physical challenges, such as slicing "flying targets with a lightsaber" with more personalised choices on the way. Eliminating the risk of ridiculing oneself in the gym or tiring the user out by long commuting to the physical space, VR workout solutions have also been proven to be as effective as regular training sessions (Hunter, 2022).

In aspects where VR workouts were not as advantageous due to the absence of the right headset equipment or personal health conditions, the overall gamification of at-home workout experience and AR equipment, meant to mix the physical realm and virtual world minimising the dizziness effects, have become just the right servitization aspect. For instance, the company called Valo Motion has developed a set of AR glasses enabling users to engage in non-conventional types of sports, such as airborne boxing, rock-climbing, and dodgeball without any sport equipment and within limited physical space. As the glasses allow the user to still be aware of the real world around, the common VR-induced issues with disorientation are easily avoidable. As such, AR workout and sports sets provide a highly entertaining and active solution for keeping up with the exercises during self-isolation.

CONCLUSION

In Chapter 2, we have learned about servitization, and, specifically, digital servitization trends during the pandemic by overviewing the cases of business innovation in the medicine and healthcare sectors, as well as the most offline industry that is manufacturing. Finally, we have identified the cases of AR and VR-based servitization among such sectors, as clothing retail and fitness industries, where the at-home virtual customer experience was proven to be even more customisable and personalised than the offline version.

REFERENCES

Pierce, D. (2020). Talkspace was built for a moment like this pandemic *protocol.* Available From: https://www.protocol.com/manuals/health-care-revolution/talkspace-was-built-for-a-moment-like-this-pan demicAccessed on July 9

Koonin, L.M., Hoots, B., Tsang, C.A., Leroy, Z., Farris, K., Jolly, B., Antall, P., McCabe, B., Zelis, C.B.R., Tong, I., Harris, A.M. (2020). Trends in the use of telehealth during the emergence of the COVID-19 pandemic—united states, January–March 2020. *MMWR Morb. Mortal. Wkly. Rep., 69*(43), 1595-1599. [http://dx.doi.org/10.15585/mmwr.mm6943a3] [PMID: 33119561]

Pancani, L., Marinucci, M., Aureli, N., Riva, P. (2021). Forced social isolation and mental health: A study on 1006 italians under COVID-19 quarantine. *Front. Psychol., 12*, 663799. [http://dx.doi.org/10.3389/fpsyg.2021.663799] [PMID: 34093358]

Hunter, T. (2022). Are VR apps for oculus a good workout? *washington post* Available From: https://www.washingtonpost.com/technology/2022/04/21/vr-workout-games/Accessed on April 21

CHAPTER 3

Creating Customer-Oriented Online-Offline Business Models

Abstract: In this chapter, we will clarify the importance of the right service design for offline-online business models under PSS. The chapter will also overview the main principles of service design. Lastly, we will become familiar with specific frameworks for driving the workflow of creating a highly customer-oriented business model through the core ideas of service design.

Keywords: Business model, Customer-oriented service, Customer journey map, Delivery gap, Service design, Service blueprint, User persona.

INTRODUCTION

As can be seen from the previous chapters, it is crucial for an innovative firm to catch upon and satisfy customers' needs, dictated by the ever-growing world changes, through more flexible forms of business models, such as PSS. Now, the essential question to ask is how exactly a firm can ensure it creates a product-service business model, which is customer- and user-oriented. While thinking of the previously discussed cases of virtual workout and telemedicine services, we have to remember that customer-oriented service design is the stepping stone to any business model success, not limited to solely global and online realms of international conglomerates. In fact, with the intense competition rising each day in all the spheres concerning both intangible services and physical products, each firm, especially small and mid-size ones, is at risk of drowning under the weight of their self-acclaimed knowledge of their consumers and their specific needs. As such, a study on a small-sized hotel in Bangkok showed the level of importance of navigating the customer-oriented service requirements in order to successfully challenge the "competition with mid and large-sized hotels" in Thailand, where international hotel chains share the majority of the market share. It was identified that customer satisfaction and loyalty are to be driven by the right strategy for designing the service products.

To put it more intuitively, whereas over 80% of companies are absolutely convinced they deliver the "superior [service] experience" to their customers, only

8% of their actual customers agree with the statement. Such a drastic difference between perception and reality can be largely attributed to and identified via the Service Gap Model, which has been discussed in Chapter 1. This is, in fact, a perfect example of the Delivery Gap, which can be explained through two major reasons: the basic business growth paradox and customer relationship difficulty. The first issue is highly difficult to overcome for any firm aiming at fast and effective growth as in pursuit of a new larger customer group, the firm innately alienates itself from the core *existing* customers, wearing off customer loyalty. For instance, if a small-sized hotel in Bangkok decides to advertise as an all-inclusive type of resort, while not offering this exact service, thus misleading their customers as the latter would expect to receive a service promoted. The second cause of the Delivery Gap is, on the other hand, the one most firms deal with and attempt at solving on a daily basis. It is generally considered that the getting-to-know-the-customer and adjustment-making are parts of a cyclical process of running a customer-oriented business model, where "get[ting] out and look[ing] [at customers' wants]" through continuous runs of user analyses is the ultimate answer to building sustainable PSS customers desire.

Although a firm utilising the Service Gap Model framework is likely to swiftly uncover and close the gaps, this is not to say that such a service design Delivery Gap cannot be ultimately avoided overall. In this sense, the specifically adjusted and customer-targeted service design becomes the major point for ensuring and improving the most sophisticated consumer experience. Service design, in its essence, should be built upon smooth communication of specific parts of the firm: business initiatives and goals, technology and market, and user analysis and understanding. Only then the firm is able to claim they are able to provide the "superior experience" as most firms do without necessarily meeting their customers' needs and uncovering their pain points.

In this Chapter, we will clarify the importance of the right service design for offline-online business models under PSS. The Chapter will also overview the main principles of service design. Lastly, we will become familiar with specific frameworks for driving the workflow of creating a highly customer-oriented business model through the core ideas of service design.

CUSTOMER EXPERIENCE: UNDERSTANDING THE IMPORTANCE

Generally speaking, customer experience is usually associated with more traditional marketing and sales touchpoints with customers, which can be overviewed under the Customer Journey Map. One of the simple examples of such traditional touchpoints can be a visually appealing physical store decoration, which is meant to catch the eye of passersby. As can be expected, before the PSS business models started developing rapidly, such purely physical customer experience initiatives have proven to be effective in bringing solid customer retention and acquisition, in turn increasing sales and loyalty. However, as digital platforms and e-commerce have started spreading around, intangible and almost fleeting interactions and impressions of a firm have started leaving a more prolonged effect on the customer experience.

In this sense, falsely, customer retention can be valued as more important than customer acquisition. However, in fact, providing the right necessary customer experience not only improves the existing consumers' loyalty but also raises brand awareness and its favourable image, which in turn generates additional consumer flows. That is due to the fact that while only 15 people tend to tell others about a satisfactory service received, a total of 24 tell about a negative experience of interacting with a firm. Thus, the importance of a positive customer experience, which ensures addressing all the essential customers' pain points, cannot be possibly diminished as it encompasses the end value of the business the customer interacts with directly.

SERVICE DESIGN: THE PRINCIPLES

Service Design, then, is an innate part of building the necessary customer experience internally from the firm and its capacities. Service Design refers to a creative and practical process, which aids the internal team in assessing, improving, and innovating the existing service or enhancing the creation of a new one. The core of Service Design is the consumer and their pain points, where the business intends to implement the changes to best meet the needs of the customers. Service Design enables the firm to deliver customer-oriented services that lead to overall business success, based on an empathetic understanding of all consumer requirements. It is, then, especially important in online-offline hybrid business models, where the right customer experience has to be ensured along both the digital and physical journey of the consumer from the very beginning stage of interactions with the brand to the ending stage of the customer receiving the end product service.

The 5 basic principles of Service Design were outlined by Marc Stickdorn and Jakob Schneider, which, first and foremost, emphasizes the user (customer)-centric approach to the process. This means the Service Design process should take into consideration all the customers' values, beliefs, preferences and even expectations regarding the product service and how they intend to use it. To gather such information on the existing customers, it is possible to conduct an extensive user analysis through rounds of surveys, personal interviews, observations and field research. Moreover, the insights coming from the inner team, such as management and other employees, can also be taken into account as they can further solidify the appointed strategy in optimising the customer experience through the given resources. Such an all-round approach should enable the firm to provide a superior type of customer experience to ensure the firm is leading the way in the innovative industry.

The next principle of the Service Design proposed is the importance of co-creation, where all the stakeholders should be involved in the process. Co-creation means not simply engaging all the members of the process in the design part of the solution but in its actual development and production. As such, multidisciplinary teams are desirable to be formed in order to ensure the inclusion of all levels of the organisation's hierarchy and customers themselves to offer all the available ranges of expertise and knowledge in the generation of ideas. Engaging all the potential actors in the Service Design process promotes a high level of consistency and commitment to customers as the centre of the service philosophy. Co-creation also guarantees that those who use the service, and those who provide it, feel valued.

Another principle of Service Design, which is referred to as the process iteration, has been briefly touched upon as the cyclic nature of a PSS business model has been discussed. As such, it is inevitable for a business to go through multiple rounds of trials and errors before landing on the perfect solution, which is expected to be continuously modified and solidified further as well. Customers can be involved in the co-creation and iteration directly through user tests of the service-product solution at any stage of the design and production process as the firm prepares new low- or high-fidelity prototypes of the potential product service. It not only further improves the understanding of the customers and their expectation when using the solution itself, but also significantly reduces the firm's financial resources, which could be wasted on a wrong and unnecessary proposition.

The next principle of Service Design is the ability of communicating through visual aids rather than pure words in order to foster the mutual understanding among all the stakeholders in a collaborative team environment. The usage of graphs, maps, and sketches can upgrade the engagement of all layers of the firm and emphasise the essential parts of the process without burdening the actors with heavy technical details.

Lastly, the Service Design process should take into consideration the whole environment in which the potential PSS exists and is expected to be delivered. As such, a holistic approach to the process is required in order to overview the whole customer journey and consider each touchpoint and pain point. Such an all-around approach can be achieved through the usage of such frameworks as Customer Persona, Service Blueprint and Customer Journey Map to highlight different customer perspectives. Through this, the firm is also able to ensure the functionality, safety and reliability of the proposed solution.

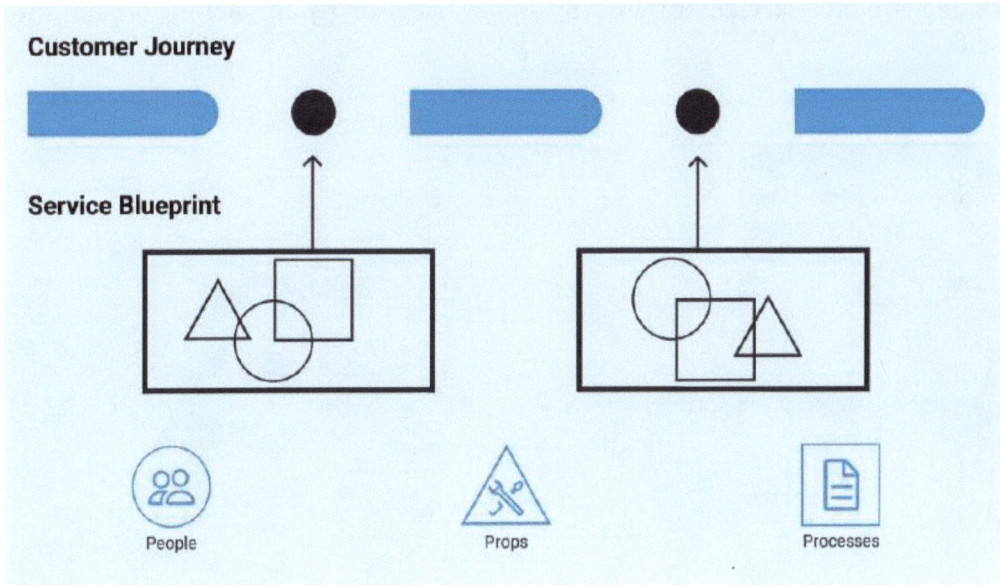

Fig. (6). The Key Components of Service Design.

All in all, Service Design in PSS models stands upon the foundation of 3 grand blocks of people, props (hardware and software), and processes, which all attribute to the process' ending solution success (Fig. **6**).

SERVICE DESIGN: PROCESS AND FRAMEWORKS

Now that we have gained a deeper understanding of what service design is and why it is important for an online-offline PSS, it is essential to understand how the process flows. Overall, there are 4 key phases in Service Design: Research, Ideate, and Prototype, which all aid the firm in getting to know its customers and delivering the customer-oriented solution the consumers want.

Before jumping right into the ideation for the PSS, it is important to set the future vision of the solution and focus on aligning the inner resources to external customers' pain points. This is to say it is crucial to specify and deliver the understanding of why a firm is embarking upon the project to all the stakeholders engaged. This stage is where the co-creation and user-centricity principles of

Service Design become the innate stimuli for mapping out the current solutions in the market or within the firm and their drawbacks from the customer perspective. To ensure the correctness of the process, the customers have to be engaged directly through surveys, field studies, interviews, which could provide the organisation with valuable insights on how a typical consumer interacts with the existing product-services offered by other firms or by the acting organisation itself.

Persona

Fig. (7). An Example of Persona Description.

In this sense, outlining a general, broad vision of a User (Consumer) Persona is an essential first step in synthesising the user research the firm is required to administer in the initial stages of Service Design (Fig. 7). Having collected a sufficient amount of insights and information from the customers, the business is able to create a Persona, which is a research-based one-page document that summarises a typical consumer/user for the top target customer groups of the product-service. The number of Personas varies based on how many target consumer groups the business is aiming at, but should not be above a total number of 3 as the greater variety of a "typical" consumer is identified, the less likely the firm is to actually extract meaningful insights from their Customer Journey. For online-offline business models of the PSS, gathering data and gaining insights from their customers is a rather natural and straightforward process as their physical presence is tightly connected to the digital platforms, where such tools as

CRM can act as an automatic tool for facilitating data collection. Persona, then, can help the acting team to emphasise the audiences' needs, biases and motivations, resulting in a more all-round understanding of their experience.

The Persona framework generally consists but is not restricted to the following elements:

A. Personal Information - including name, gender, age, occupation, location and photo for a more visual approach;

B. Description or Biography - a short explanation of what the customer does and what their main focus is in interacting with the product-service;

C. Motivation, Influences - a brief list of points that explain what exactly is driving the Persona's actions and choices;

D. Goals or Needs - the top three to five high-level things that this Persona finds necessary to accomplish;

E. Pain Points - the top three to five worries that this Persona has when interacting with the existing solutions or given the lack of them;

F. Main quote - a compelling quote that summarises the Persona's immediate needs or perspective;

G. Service Usage - most frequently used services that are not limited to the target industry, showcasing the willingness to interact with digital business models;

Persona, although containing some imaginative parts, such as the customer's name and photo, should be based on a data- and research-driven summary of all the users the firm has a chance to directly interact with. As such, the importance of the customer research is emphasised once again.

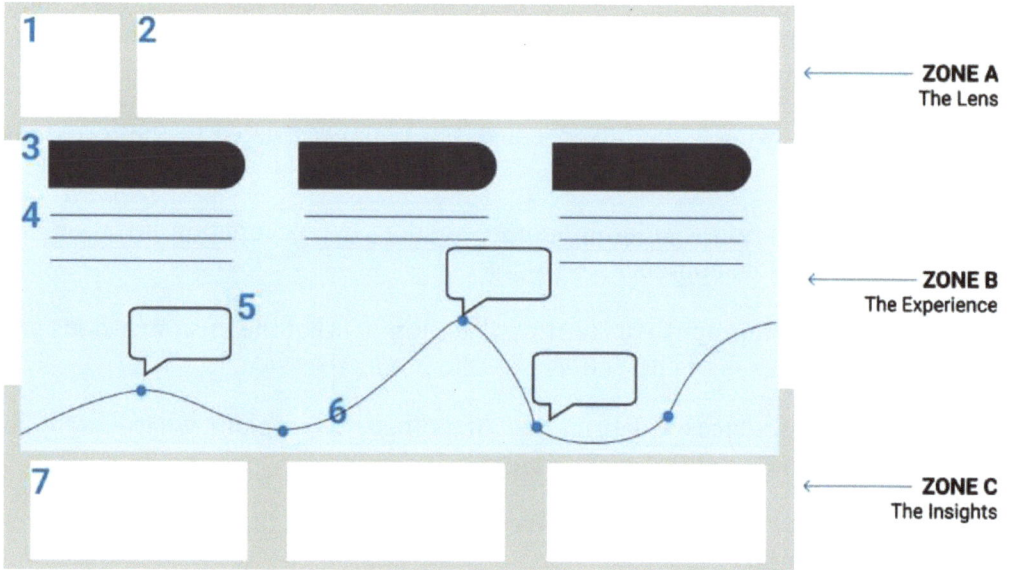

Fig (8). An Example of Customer Journey Mapping.

Once the firm identifies its typical Customer Personas, it is possible to outline this Persona's Customer Journey (Fig. **8**). Journey mapping starts by combining a series of consumer goals and actions into a timeline, which is based on the customer's thoughts and emotions creating a simulation of a real-life narrative. Finally, such a narrative is summarised visually to communicate insights that will inform further Service Design processes. Storytelling and efficient visualisation are crucial parts of the Customer Journey map as they effectively and concisely convey the information and insights received via user research, creating a shared vision of the entire customer experience for all the firm stakeholders. This shared vision is a critical aim of journey mapping as with the lack of it, the internal business agreement on how to improve customer experience simply does not occur.

The Customer Journey Map framework generally consists of but is not restricted to the following zones:

A. The lens provides constraints for the map by assigning (1) a Persona, which is identified through the Persona framework, and (2) the scenario to be examined;

B. The heart of the map is the visual experience, aligned across (3) time-based phases of the journey: the (4) actions, (5) thoughts, and (6) emotional experience can be included;

C. The output should vary based on the business goal the map supports, but it could describe the insights and pain points discovered, and the (7) opportunities to focus on going forward, as well as internal ownership.

The main advantage of creating a Customer Journey Map for better Service Design is its end goal of shifting the firm's perspective from inside-out to outside-in, namely making the product service more customer-oriented. Journey mapping sheds light on real human experiences that often organisations own limited knowledge about. The map should also prioritise aligning the touchpoints and channels (methods of communication or service delivery, such as the website or physical store) with customer needs and actions (Kaplan, 2016).

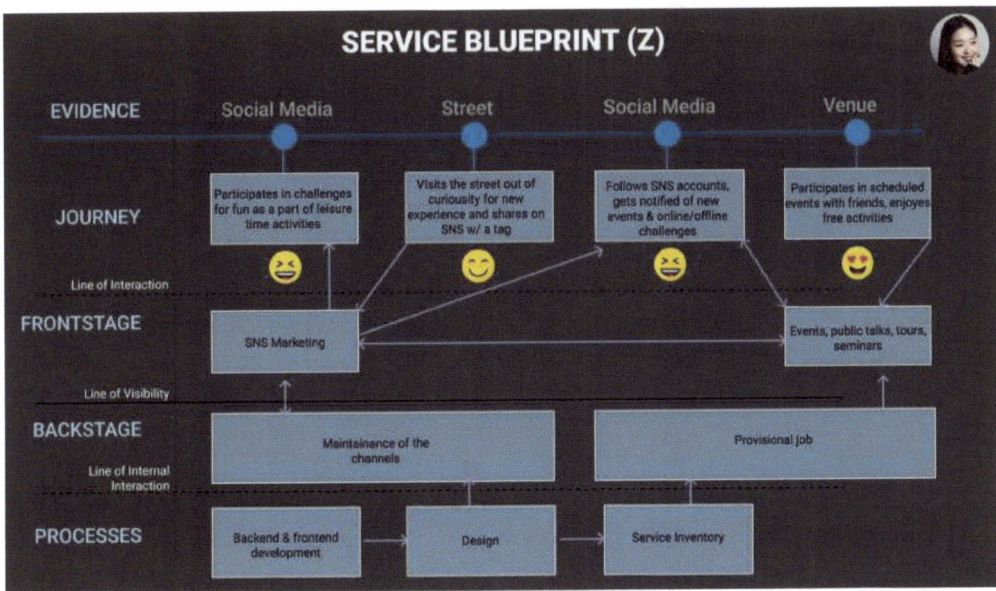

Fig. (9). An Example of Service Blueprint.

Service Blueprint

Having completed the outside customer perspective and their journey when interacting with the product-service or other solutions, it is now possible to implement the primary tool of the Service Design process, which is the Service (Fig. **9**). Service Blueprint allows the team to plan and organise the firm's resources (people, props, and processes) in order to improve the customer's experience. In its essence, it is a diagram, which depicts the relationships between different service components — people, props (physical or digital evidence), and processes — that are directly tied to touchpoints in a specific customer journey, which we have discussed in the previous section. As such, it is possible to think of the Service Blueprint as a natural continuation of the Customer Journey Map. The Blueprint corresponds to a specific single customer journey and the specific Persona, whose journey is identified. Thus, for the same product-service solution, there can be a number of Blueprints for several different scenarios.

Service Blueprints are especially valuable in helping the business identify and solve their solution's weakness, where the customer experience is at its poorest performance. In this same way, blueprints help identify opportunities for optimization as the visualisation of the relationships uncovers potential improvements and ways to eliminate redundancy.

The Service Blueprint framework generally consists of but is not restricted to the following elements:

A. Customer Actions (Customer Journey)

B. Frontstage Action

C. Backstage Action

D. Processes

As for the Customer Actions, this part of the Service Blueprint is largely revolving around the previously overviewed framework of the Customer Journey Map. On the other hand, the Frontstage, Backstage Action and Processes elements are crucial to discuss in depth. Firstly, the Frontstage section of the Blueprint refers to those actions, which are visible to the customer and occur directly in front of them. These actions can vary in forms from human-to-human to human-to-computer interactions and non-target actions. Human-to-human actions are the activities, where a specific employee performs certain tasks (*e.g.*, posting social media promotional content), while human-to-computer ones are conducted with the usage of self-service technology, such as ATMs or kiosks in physical stores. As for the Backstage actions, these are the activities that occur behind the scenes to support the front stage actions directly. These actions could be administered and performed by a backstage employee (*e.g.*, maintenance of the website by a back-end engineer), whose work is not directly seen by the consumers. Finally, the processes are internal to the firm interactions and actions, which support the business in delivering the product-service.

In the Blueprint framework, the aforementioned elements are carefully organised into clusters with 3 lines that separate them: 1) line of interaction, which visualises the direct interactions between the inner team and external customers, 2) line of visibility, separating non-visible and visible to the consumer actions, 3) line of internal interaction, differentiating employees who engage in direct communication with the customers and those who do not. Moreover, there is a layer called Evidence, which is made of the props and places that anyone in the blueprint has an exchange with based on the Customer Journey Map. Last but not least, connecting arrows are a key element of the Blueprint as they indicate relationships and dependencies within the whole flow in-between the customer and the business. A single arrow suggests a one-way interaction or exchange, while a double arrow pinpoints the codependency.

To diversify and actually extend the Service Blueprint framework to gain more valuable insights, additional elements, such as time variables, regulations, emotions and metrics, can be included.

Overall, the Service Blueprint is a crucial tool in creating the right Service Design for an online-offline business model as it essentially helps the firm to see the big picture of how a product-service is implemented internally and is used by the customers externally. Service Design, based on the Service Blueprint, pinpoints crucial dependencies between employee-facing and customer-facing processes in a visually coherent format and is instrumental in identifying pain points, optimising complex interactions, and ultimately saving money for the organisation and improving the experience for its customers, while also promoting a positive customer-oriented brand image.

CONCLUSION

Service design, then, focuses on how the business model, especially the one as flexible and risky as a PSS, operates and delivers the product-service it essentially promises. Each detail and mechanism play a dramatic role in shaping the whole of the customer experience, even when it is not directly visible to the consumer. In this Chapter, we have learned about the importance of forming the right customer experience through understanding and sympathizing with the core customers' needs and pain points. To ensure the delivery of such a superior experience, the firm is expected to implement the methods of user research and then, based on the data- and research-driven summaries, compile a full big picture of their consumers and how they tend to interact with the proposed solution. After that, the Service Blueprint framework becomes the sophisticated tool for ensuring the alignment of internal processes and actions to the external customers' needs (Gibbons, 2017).

REFERENCES

Gibbons, S. (2017). Service design 101 *nielsen norman group*. Available From: https://www.nngroup.com/articles/service-design-101/Accessed on July 9

Kaplan, K. (2016). When and how to create customer journey maps *nielsen norman group*. Available From: https://www.nngroup.com/articles/customer-journey-mapping/Accessed on July 13

CHAPTER 4

Technology-Service Convergence for Value Innovation and Social Welfare

Abstract: In this chapter, we will discuss the notion of value innovation and its importance for the PSS business models, while differentiating the areas of red and blue oceans heavily based on the winning idea of the Blue Ocean Strategy proposed by Chan Kim and Renée Mauborgne in 2004. The chapter will also overview the main strategies for getting started with value innovation for firms through differentiation. Finally, the concept is to be put into practice through the review of case studies of firms and organisations that have engaged in value innovation through redefining market boundaries.

Keywords: Blue ocean strategy, Social innovation, Technology-service convergence, Value innovation.

INTRODUCTION

In a fast-paced technology and data-driven society and industry, there is an immense potential for growth, disruption and creation of more flexible and, hence, high-risk markets and new business models. With such an advantage of continuous improvement and creation comes increasingly fierce competition, which further enhances the vulnerability of both existing firms and new entrants in the market, where the value of differentiation from competitors cannot be diminished. In a traditional sense, differentiation is driven either by increasing the value of the firm's specific offer or by simply pursuing a cost-saving or low-price strategy, which enforces a head-to-head competition based majorly on incremental improvements in cost, quality, or both. As such, the majority of the organizations opt between either value or pricing, while completely alienating themselves from the concept of breaking the value-cost trade-off, where value innovation becomes the stepping stone to the company's success (Porumboiu, 2021).

While most companies focus on matching or even getting ahead of their rivals, such pursuit often leads to similar actions undertaken and strategies alike, which essentially cancel out the differentiation goal. Instead, Chan Kim and Renée Mauborgne in their book on the Blue Ocean Strategy shed light on innovative firms' tactics, which isolate themselves from the rest of the market by building out fundamentally new competition-free market space by creating flexible forms of product services. Such a path to value innovation requires a competitive mindset and a systematic way of not simply identifying market opportunities in customers' needs, but also driving them. Instead of searching within the conventional boundaries of the current industry competition, innovation-oriented firms are able to look methodically beyond those invisible limitations to find deserted areas of the market that represent real value innovation.

Kim and Mauborgne identified that the major reason why specific firms grow in a sustainable manner at a fast pace unlike their competitors is due to their contrasting approaches to framing strategies. The difference in approaches was not caused by a detailed choice of a specific tool or model, but rather by the firm's fundamental and implicit assumptions about strategy and why exactly they were pursuing it. While less successful companies' strategies were dominated by the idea of staying ahead of the game, the top businesses paid little to no attention to their rivals and sought to emphasise their value proposition through value innovation. This is due to the fact that innovations are considered to be the major drivers of sustainable, steady and long-term growth for a business, especially in such a vulnerable environment as product-service systems.

In this Chapter, we will discuss the notion of value innovation and its importance for the PSS business models, while differentiating the areas of red and blue oceans heavily based on the winning idea of the Blue Ocean Strategy proposed by Chan Kim and Renée Mauborgne in 2004 (Fig. **10**). The chapter will also overview the main strategies for getting started with value innovation for firms through differentiation. Finally, the concept is to be put in practice through the review of case studies of firms and organisations, that have engaged in value innovation through redefining market boundaries.

VALUE INNOVATION: UNDERSTANDING THE CONCEPT AND BACKGROUND

Value innovation is an all-around, solid foundation of the Blue Ocean Strategy theory and framework developed by Kim and Mauborgne in their book, which proposes a methodology for innovation-oriented firms to break free from standard industry competition and explore the possibilities beyond it. The ascending questions that should be asked are then: what exactly is the Blue Ocean and are there any other Oceans the framework takes into consideration?

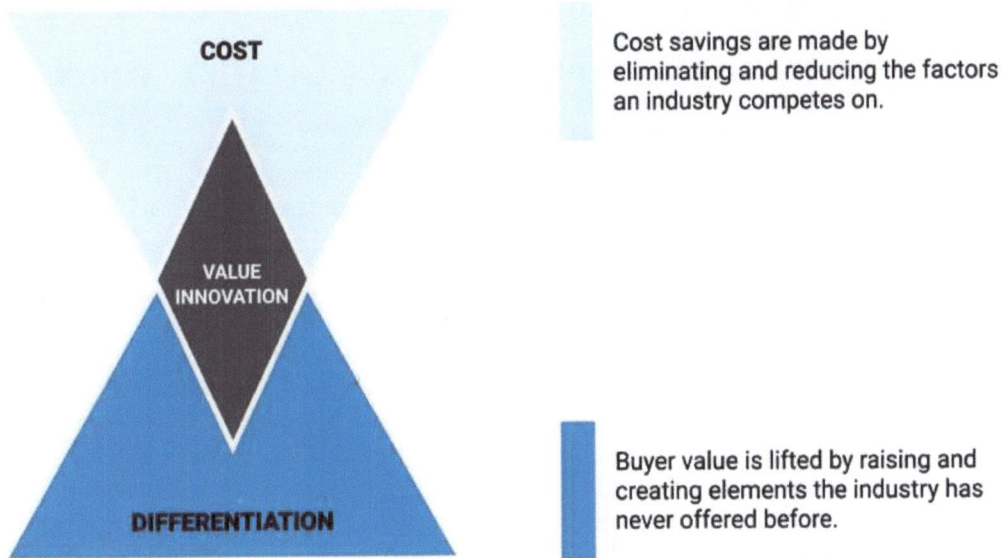

COST

Cost savings are made by eliminating and reducing the factors an industry competes on.

VALUE INNOVATION

Buyer value is lifted by raising and creating elements the industry has never offered before.

DIFFERENTIATION

Fig. (10). Value Innovation Strategy by Cost Saving and Differentiation.

Blue Oceans, according to the authors, refer to all the unexplored or unknown markets, where competition is non-existent. Thus, the Blue Ocean is full of opportunities for profitable, sustainable growth. In sharp contrast, the Red Oceans, the existing markets, are filled with the stoic and harsh competition that eliminates the opportunities for harvesting profit for new entrants and less grand players, which cannot overthrow the current top players. As such, the Blue Ocean Strategy is based on the concept of creating new demand by developing uncontested market space by disrupting or expanding the existing market instead of competing in the congested Red Ocean. This is where the notion of value innovation comes in as the major turning point of the firm's strategy.

Value Innovation is, then, the simultaneous pursuit of differentiation and low cost, where the combination of both and the creation of a new uncontested market space is essential for further success. Such a combination ensures that innovation is not internally driven by the firm's existing resources or aspirations, but provides a highly customer-oriented product-service design. Technical enhancement is the major element to review, evaluate and improve under the value innovation as an infinite number of businesses offer products and services with a variety of functions and values irrelevant to the consumer. Value Innovation, in this sense, can be considered to be administered and deployed successfully only if the firm aligns the proposed innovative product, service, or process with utility, price and cost. As a result, Value Innovation benefits both the customers and the company as it eliminates competition, ensures cost savings, and enhances the exponential mindset of the stakeholders.

VALUE INNOVATION: SHOWCASING ADVANTAGES THROUGH REAL-LIFE CASES

For instance, a traditional example of a successful Value Innovation initiative is set all the way in the early 2000s with Nintendo successfully overthrowing the major competition in the console games industry dominated by such giants as Microsoft and Sony. Instead of pursuing the classic HD technology, which has been paving the way to the top for the latter rivals, Nintendo has put its stakes on the Nintendo Wii, which was supposed to target a new market segment of casual, non-professional gamers. Opting not to pursue the most demanding technological aspect of the existing market, Nintendo was able to lower production costs and simultaneously increase the value for the customers in their new target segment, consisting majorly of families with young children. Such a strategic decision of pursuing lower-cost technology and differentiation point has led to unfolding the story of success with Nintendo becoming the sales leader with over 100 million units sold by simply staying vigilant and not putting all on traditional technological improvement. Later, as the Nintendo Wii trend died down, Nintendo made a grand comeback with the Nintendo Switch, once again choosing to not compete with high-end PS and Xbox consoles, but rather covering the pain points of an entirely new segment, which have long been neglected.

As such, it can be seen that Value Innovation allows the firm to grasp the harvest of higher value at a lower cost. To put it more intuitively, another example of a successful implementation of Value Innovation is the Accor company and its Formule 1 range of hotels. Accor has opted to reject the costly features of additional "luxurious" space, such as 24/7 receptions, lobby, big closets, and desks in order to ensure their service satisfies the most crucial customers' need, which is getting a good night comfortable sleep. Saving costs on building rooms and employing additional personnel allowed them to invest in what customers would value more.

Moreover, another noteworthy benefit of value innovation is the unconventional thinking that it enforces. Successful growth- and customer-focused firms tend to invest more resources into exponential value rather than incremental improvements. To put it in a simple manner, instead of focusing on how to make a 10% improvement from the previous benchmark, it is essential to shift the attention onto how to deliver a 10x better experience to the consumers. In the worst-case scenario, a company, competing with several other firms and pursuing solely incremental short-lived improvements for competitive advantage, is likely to be outperformed by a new entrant or an existing rival. However, Value

Innovation and exponential thinking open up a whole new path not simply outperforming, but breaking free from the stoic market.

One classic example of such an unconventional mindset in regard to Value Innovation has been depicted in the 1960s to 1980s when the movie theatre industry was experiencing a harsh decline due to the rapid spread of videocassette recorders and players. As such, major cinema operators were forced to exit the market, while those, who had survived, competed intensely for the ever-downgrading market share as they "broadened their film offerings…, expanded their food and drink services, and increased showing times", which did not result in any significant returns. Instead of pursuing the same head-to-head competitive strategy, Kinepolis, the first megaplex in the world, offered a superior customer experience with a large number of screens and seats available. By doing this, Kinepolis won 50% of the market in its first year of operation and expanded the existing market by about 40% through the simple principles of Value Innovation.

VALUE INNOVATION: IMPLEMENTING

To actually discover a Blue Ocean and harvest the advantages of Value Innovation, Kim and Mauborgne suggest that businesses consider the Four Actions Framework to break the value-cost trade-off and craft a new customer value proposition (Sridharan, 2021). The Four Actions Framework in Fig. (**11**) consists of the given elements:

A. Eliminate - which of the factors does the industry take for granted that should the business eliminate?

B. Reduce - which factors should a business reduce well below the industry's standard?

C. Raise - what factors should a business raise well above the industry's standard?

D. Create - what factors should a business create that the industry has never offered?

For the 'Eliminate' requirement, it is crucial to overview and evaluate what features the market assumes of the product-service are not necessary and do not deliver any value or enhance it in any possible dimension. By removing redundant items, functions or actions, the firm is able to reduce their spending dramatically. For example, Cirque du Soleil has opted to not use animals in their performances as their target audience consisted of adults, who were not expressing specific needs for animal shows. As such, the circus was able to significantly lower its maintenance and transportation costs.

REDUCE

ELIMINATE — New Value Core — CREATE

RAISE

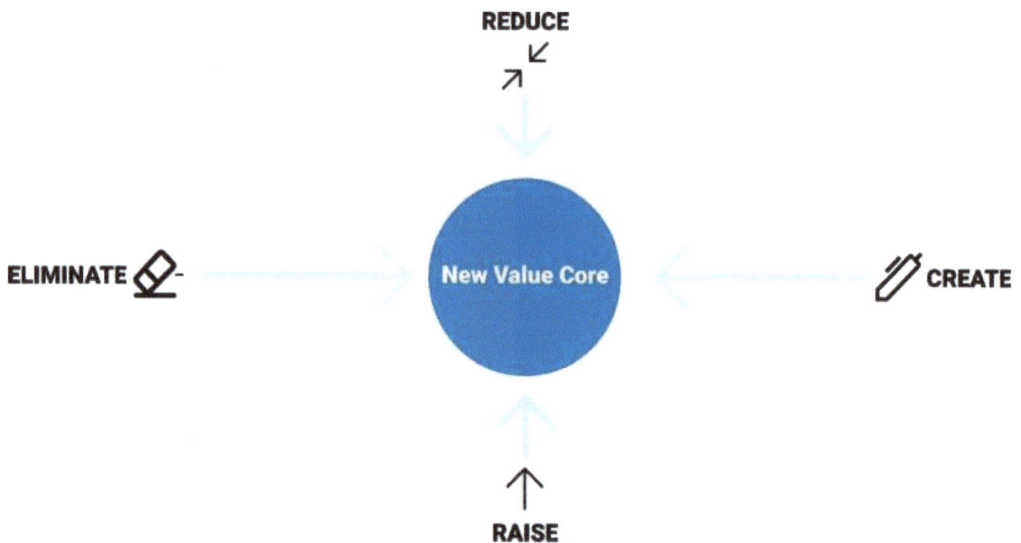

Fig. (11). Eliminate, Reduce, Raise and Create for Value Innovation.

Next, it is essential for a business to 'Reduce' features, which are below the industry standard. Although the market may still require more advanced technologies or features, the existing offerings might be well above the required necessity. An example of such an initiative can be attributed to the Nintendo Wii case, where the brand decided to develop a less advanced gaming product for average users. Instead of focusing on such advanced features as an HD screen, the firm is able to 'Raise' factors well above the industry standard to remove compromises that the existing options force customers to make. For example, Apple initiated a highly customer-oriented product-service system with its iPod by providing a proprietary platform of content for customers to rely on. Finally, the organisation is required to take upon the journey of 'Creating' features that have never been offered before in the market or engage in the process of innovating as it would add tremendous value to their product-service proposition.

HEALTHCARE VALUE AND SOCIAL INNOVATION: SOUTH KOREA'S CASE ON TRADITIONAL KOREAN MEDICINE VALUE INNOVATION

Now that we have gotten accustomed to the concept of Value Innovation and classic examples of its implementation, we are able to overview a recent case of the homecare medicine industry shift amid the COVID-19 pandemic in South

Korea. In specific, the research conducted by Sung, *et al.,* aimed to examine the status of community care services regarding traditional Korean medicine (TKM) for older adults through an in-depth examination of 16 local governments and raise awareness of current opinions and services of TKM institutions.

In response to the rapidly increasing number of COVID-19 cases and dramatically declined urgent and general access to face-to-face medical aid distributed majorly through hospitals, the government of South Korea has temporarily initiated telemedicine consultations for the specific vulnerable groups in need of constant patient care, such as the elderly, people with mental illnesses, and other disadvantaged people. However, opting not to limit the scope of urgent non-face-to-face medical assistance to online doctor appointments only, a pilot community Korean medicine homecare program has been promoted for an ageing population in specific. That is due to the fact that this group of society had already been familiar and had expressed genuine trust towards the traditional national medicine rooted deeply within Korean history and society with over 86% of elderly above 60 years old using its methods.

As such, consultation, diagnosis, education and even actual treatment,including instances of acupuncture, moxibustion, herbal medicine, chuna therapy and cupping were proposed for the elderly and other patients with impaired mobility, who were not able to attend a physical appointment or receive in-patient treatment. Ultimately promoting the type of "simple tools or hands" medicine without harsh reliance on modern equipment, which was difficult to access due to the restrictions at COVID-19 high-hazard zone areas such as hospitals, has proven to be an effective strategy for the government as it not only simplified the access to medicine and heightened the consumer value of the TKM, but also significantly reduced the diagnosis and treatment-related costs of the medical field.

This is to highlight the ultimate Value Innovation side of the program as the combination of differentiation (buyer/consumer value) points and lower cost strategies, which, eventually, have also made a significant social impact by benefiting the physical and mental welfare of the South Korean society. The results of the study showed that the average satisfaction rate of using the TKM service is 4.5 out of 5.0 points with the majority of the respondents confessing that the program has been especially helpful in regard to health. As such, covered under the national medical insurance and policies, the TKM homecare program and services could function as a viable, patient-oriented, and relatively low-cost alternative for continued medical care disrupted by the unforeseen circumstance of limited face-to-face consultations, diagnosis and treatment for people with impaired mobility and mental illnesses, as well as satisfying the target consumer group of the elderly in South Korea.

CONCLUSION

To sum it up, Value Innovation strategy is primarily founded upon the idea of pursuing differentiation and low cost, which does not take business compromises into account. In contrast to competitive strategy, which is largely focused on differentiation, focus strategy and cost advantage, value innovation strategy seeks to break the value-cost trade-off by eliminating and reducing factors an industry competes on and raising and creating factors the industry has never offered. In this Chapter, we have learned about the importance of forming the right customer experience through understanding and sympathising with the core customers' needs and pain points. To ensure the delivery of such a superior experience, the firm is expected to implement the methods of user research and then, based on the data- and research-driven summaries, compile a full big picture of their consumers and how they tend to interact with the proposed solution. After that, the Service Blueprint framework becomes the sophisticated tool for ensuring the alignment of internal processes and actions to the external customers' needs (Gibbons, 2017).

REFERENCES

Porumboiu, D. (2021). What is value innovation and why does it matter? *viima* Available From: https://www.viima.com/blog/value-innovationAccessed on September 6

Sridharan, M. (2021). Value innovation: How to construct a blue ocean strategy? *think insights* Available From: https://thinkinsights.net/strategy/value-innovation/Accessed on January 19

CHAPTER 5

Exemplary Cases of Servitization for Overcoming Crisis

Abstract: As demonstrated in Chapters 1-4, the notions of servitization and PSS are currently becoming the new normal for businesses all over the world, especially in the unfolded circumstances of the pandemic and the gradual transition to online digital space. To further aggregate the theoretical frameworks discussed, this chapter will introduce a number of relevant winning cases of the implementation of servitization and PSS models among the platform giants in travel and stay booking, e-commerce, car sharing, content, as well as health appliance and telemedicine industries.

Keywords: Crisis-induced servitization, E-commerce service, Manufacturing servitization, Virtual travelling.

INTRODUCTION

Coupang: E-Commerce Services Pandemic Boom

When it comes to COVID-19, it is an undeniable truth that the restrictions and the following crisis have halted or at least restrained the majority of global economic activities and, thereby, significantly damaged industries and created economic shock as a large international ripple effect. According to the OECD (2020), a month of quarantine reduces the annual rate of GDP by as much as 2%. As such, since the Korean economy is highly dependent on international trade being "one of the world's most export-dependent industrialised nations", Korea could not avoid severe damages from the abrupt termination of the global commerce flux. In response, Korea has been able to push forward those domestic industries that managed to turn the limitations into an opportunity for rapid growth. The top four South Korean companies that have successfully expanded during COVID-19, as pointed out in the previous Chapters, are online shopping and delivery services, which further demonstrates the general trend of seeking remote purchasing options in the post-pandemic society. Among the four winners, Coupang stands out as a firm that made the most exponential progress due to its innovative tactics and strategic moves in servitization. The case successfully highlights the methods of how the business can recognize necessary components to attract investment and utilise the existing assets to face unsystematic risks, such as the pandemic.

Overall, there are multiple factors Coupang considered to efficiently structure its value chain to maximise profits in the unexpected events of the COVID-19 crisis. Firstly, as for the personalised approach to customers, Coupang realised that its users' main complaint is a long period of delivery. Having identified such a pain point among its major shortcomings, Coupang developed new delivery services, such as Rocket Delivery, Rocket WOW and Rocket Fresh all aimed at not simply reducing but majorly cutting down on the waiting time for its most valued customers. While the Rocket Delivery program is intended to bring the customers' products based on zero additional delivery fee based on the minimum required purchase sum, the Rocket WOW subscription allows the users to order unlimited purchase amounts. Rocket Fresh, on the other hand, provides a service of overnight delivery of fresh groceries that is essential for the majority of South Korean households. The fast delivery services, however, only became possible due to the company's initiative of launching fulfillment services and contracting the logistics providers as it allowed a large amount and variety of products to be instantly prepared and shipped.

Furthermore, to provide a broader range of products and reach out to a wider user range, Coupang implemented Rocket Earth, an initiative to ensure the provision of unavailable Korean items from all over the world, which effectively covered the pain point of the customers, who are unable to travel and shop abroad or initiate purchases on foreign e-commerce platforms due to the language barrier. As a result of such strategic moves amid the pandemic, Coupang gained a solid layer of new customers, leading to a dramatic increase in product sales - the main component of the firm's revenue stream. All in all, by effectively analysing its weaknesses, listening to the customers' pain points, and launching newer and more efficient services, Coupang has managed to innovate the outdated delivery system through servitization and personalised customer approach by reflecting both the market trends, as well as the circumstances of the current world, which led to the rise of the company's revenue to the rate of over $11 billion in 2020, a 45% increase from the revenue level of 2019.

MY REAL TRIP: SHIFTING TRAVEL PLATFORMS FOCUS TO VIRTUAL & DOMESTIC ROUTES

While greatly promoting the industries related to the online space, such as e-commerce, the pandemic has, on the other hand, critically affected various other businesses, including the tourism industry highly dependent on the physical presence of customers and their ability to commute internationally. According to the report of the United Nations World Tourism Organization, the number of international tourists in the world decreased by roughly 75% in 2020 compared to 2019. For South Korea especially, the damage to the travel industry reached a critical point of approximately 86% drop in the number of incoming foreign travelers. Statistically, according to the Korea Association of Travel Agents, more than 4,000 travel-related companies were virtually closed due to the imposed restrictions with the majority of the survivors struggling to find methods to stay afloat and break even.

One such company My Real Trip, a travel-oriented booking platform, has suffered significant financial losses and has had to define and initiate innovative strategies to revive its business from crisis. In general, My Real Trip pursued two servitization initiatives amid the pandemic: 1) transforming "the paradigm of travel" and 2) pivoting the focus of their travel services. As for the first strategy, the company decided to turn its customers' pain point of inability to travel into a demand stream by developing a live tour service, which allowed the users to embark upon a guided virtual trip via a YouTube live stream, where "tourists" were able to actively engage in communication with the tour guides through the functions of commenting, liking and reacting to the stream, which significantly elevated the notion of the customised approach of the company. As for the second initiative, My Real Trip proactively shifted the focus from international travelling to domestic tours among its customers after thorough research and data analysis findings that hinted at the people's willingness to switch to the exploration of domestic routes. Based on such demand, My Real Trip launched various home travel packages in South Korea, including over 3,000 tours to Jeju Island, which it successfully advertised on social media platforms to reach more than 5% more of its target clientele of MZ Generation. As a result of servitization methods and recognising customers' needs, My Real Trip managed to overcome the physical travel-related barriers imposed by the pandemic and subdue financial and business challenges.

RIDI BOOKS: FORMING LONG-TERM CUSTOMER RELATIONSHIPS BASED ON PSS

RIDI Books, a connected content company, turned into a surplus with the highest performance amid the pandemic, recording a 35% year-on-year growth with a total of 155.6 billion Korean won in 2020 and an operating profit of 2.6 billion Korean won. As such, RIDI became one of the Korean unicorns that hold a value of more than one trillion won despite the pandemic circumstances. Although the book market is highly regressive due to its outdated strategies, RIDI has been growing rapidly in the past 10 consecutive years by targeting ebook markets and effectively establishing a PSS business model through its unique content curation service.

To be more precise, RIDI started its business as an ebook provider jumping onto the window of opportunities created by the fall of sales among physical books. The major problem faced by the company, however, was also caused by the paper book market as customers were looking for methods to not simply find and purchase a specific book title, but also leaf through the shelves and come across unexpected findings without actually purchasing the paper book, which was highly difficult on ebook platforms. Having identified the pain point of book readers, RIDI initiated its RIDI Select subscription-based service, which allowed customers to read an unlimited amount of titles freely without the burden of the actual purchase by emphasising the actual reading experience as a whole. By paying less than $7 a month, RIDI readers are able to access the full library of contents, including magazines and webtoons, as well as have suggestions based on the previous titles added through the curation model. The servitization initiative greatly diversified the approach to customers at RIDI and, thus, added value to the products offered and differentiated it from similar ebook providers. As a result, RIDI Select's servitization strategies led to a stronger customer-centricity, which allowed RIDI to transform its business from a transaction-based one to a relationship-based platform.

COWAY: COMBINING HEALTH APPLIANCES MANUFACTURING AND SERVICES

Coway is a company specialising in environmental home appliances such as water purifiers, air purifiers, bidets, and water softeners since it was founded in 1989. In 1998, Coway introduced the concept of a rental business for the first time in the industry and is providing customers with a differentiated service called Cody-On Service through "Cody," a service expert. Cody, the abbreviation for Coway Lady, is a specialist directly employed by Coway to perform maintenance tasks for the customers. During the 1998 IMF financial Crisis, Coway was suffering from financial difficulties. It was also the time when Coway made the significant decision to change its business model from the door-to-door business model to the rental business model. At that time, its competitors guaranteed that the rental service would fail because it was a sales method that goes against the trend. However, the rental services were the solution that saved the company as during the recession, customers could not afford to purchase water purifiers worth more than 1 million won. According to the survey conducted by Coway, Korean consumers prefer renting a water purifier to buying it by a ratio of 4 to 1. Eventually, being the first in the industry to start the rental business model has enabled Coway to establish strong brand recognition and customer loyalty. Coway achieved about 500% sales growth from 2000 until 2009 (Coway, 2023).

Another success factor of Coway's PSS is the high quality of service. For drinking water quality, a water purifier requires preventive maintenance including hose and inner water tank cleaning, and filter replacement, all of which require a high service frequency. Coway is currently providing safe services to customers with 14,000 CODYs and 1,500 AS experts, who contribute the most to satisfying customers by visiting them periodically. Coway has started the Cody-On Service for 24 hours a day to continuously communicate with customers and request information, including inspection schedules, records, and user manuals without limitations in time and space. Coway also adopted counseling through an online texting platform KakaoTalk to further improve accessibility and convenience. Through a 2-month regular service, CODYs ensure the cleanliness and hygiene of the Coway products. Coway requires CODYs to go through professional training, exams, and follow-up practices to improve the quality of service and enhance customer satisfaction. As a result, Coway was selected as the top company in the water purifier and air purifier sector in 2018.

CONCLUSION

In this Chapter, we analysed the winning servitization cases in detail, as well as highlighted the necessity to differentiate offline business models through services in order to overcome unsystematic risks and crises and overcome financial and business stagnation through the usage of minimal additional physical assets.

ACKNOWLEDGMENT

This research was supported by Soonchunhyang University's research project #2021-0922. The author also acknowledges the students' assistance in preparing the manuscript.

REFERENCES

Coway. (2023). *Coway filter maintenance & services.* Available From: https://www.coway.com.my/ heartserviceAccessed on 26th February

OECD. (2020). *Tax and fiscal policy in response to the coronavirus crisis: strengthening confidence and resilience.* Available From: https://www.oecd.org/coronavirus/policy-responses/tax-and-fiscal-poli-y-in-response-to-th e-coronavirus-crisis-strengthening-confidence-and-resilience-60f640a8/

SUBJECT INDEX

A

Abnormality score 19
Accor company 40
Actions 34, 41
  framework 41
  human-to-human 34
  non-target 34
Actors, potential 28
Acupuncture 43
Aerospace engine 1
Ageing population 43
AI-powered solution 20
Air purifiers 48
Airborne boxing 23
Airlines 1, 11
Aligning customers 8
Alignment of internal processes and actions
    35, 44
Amazon's Alexa 7
Amid 22, 42, 46, 47
  highest performance 47
  homecare medicine industry shift 42
  virtual stores 22
Apple's Siri assistance 19
Approach 18, 20, 28, 31, 46
  cost-saving 20
  holistic 28
  personalised customer 46
  traditional 18
  visual 31
AR 22, 23, 24
  and VR-based servitization 24
  equipment 23
  glasses 23
  solution 22
  workout 23
Aspirations 39
Assets 3, 14, 46, 49
  intangible 3, 14
  physical 49
Automated 17, 19, 22

diagnosis platforms 19
diagnostics solutions 19
virtual in-store consultancy 22
Automation processes 17
Automobile manufacturing brands 21

B

Big data capabilities 19
Biofourmis platform 20
Blue Ocean 41
  and harvest 41
Blue Ocean strategy 37, 38, 39
  theory and framework 38
Blueprint 34, 35
  framework 34
  help 34
BMW 21
Boundaries, redefining market 37, 38
Brand 27, 48
  awareness 27
  recognition, strong 48
Building revenue streams 21
Burberry 22
Business 2, 3, 4, 5, 6, 7, 8, 12, 14, 15, 23,
27, 28, 30, 33, 34, 35, 41, 46, 48, 49
  goal 33
  innovation 14, 15, 23
  profitability 2
  rental 48
  stagnation 49
  success 27
Business models 12, 16, 18, 20, 21, 25, 26, 27,
    30, 31, 35, 48
  customer-oriented 25, 26
  digital 31
  door-to-door 48
  hybrid 27
  innovative 18
  offline-online 25, 26
  online-offline 30, 35
  rental 48